A Tale of Twin Cities

A Tale of Twin Cities

GROWING UP IN MENOMINEE

Mary Lynn Hall

ISBN-13: 9781537131160
ISBN-10: 1537131168

A Tale of Twin Cities

The glow of stadium lights could be seen above the roof of the high school. On a crisp Saturday a capacity crowd of maroon and white and purple and white clad fans cheered as the oldest interstate high school rivalry in the country played out. Even in grade school we took our turn standing in line to buy tickets for the M&M game.

Twin cities, Marinette, Wisconsin, and Menominee, Michigan, were really just one big playground for the gang of kids who grew up in my hometowns. We bused around the loop, rode bikes to Menominee's Ideal Dairy or the Marinette Produce for double dip ice cream cones and ultimately drove the family Pontiac or Ford across the interstate, Hattie Street or Menekaunee Bridge.

In grade school we were devoted to Saturday movies at the Menominee Opera House. We paid a quarter and waited for years to watch Roy Rogers kiss Dale Evans. During the week we relived our favorite scenes mounting our Schwinn steeds and riding between our ranches, Peggy Paitl and Elaine Moses' garages. St. Anne's school grounds, which stood in the middle of our block, was the perfect spot to gather for round up or whatever adventure beckoned us to the range. We wore holsters and sported six shooters. The ultimate birthday present for me was a pair of cowboy boots that I wish I still had. When not engaged in Western warfare, half of us staged plays and charged the other half a nickel to attend. They took place in an orchard next to Josephson's house on Dunlap Avenue. We often left home after breakfast and returned in time for dinner with no phone calls or other parental contact except for those who watched quietly from their windows.

Victory gardens were popular and on early summer evenings Mr. Paitl would slice a fresh kohlrabi for us to taste. Mrs. Paitl, Peggy's mom, often cooked for events at the Bohemian Hall and we sampled cookies, casseroles, kolaches and whatever else she prepared. To this day the recipe for Mrs. Paitl's hot dish is tucked into my recipe box. When WWII ended, Peggy's dad put away the pairing knife and pulled out his trombone to lead the neighborhood in a triumphant march around the block.….right down the middle of the street.

I have to laugh when I think of packing cars or campers to drive to Door County or Eagle River. We jumped on our bikes and headed downtown to Victory or Memorial Beach or out to Henes Park. Day camp was held each summer at the Wells House on the waterfront where we learned to swim and make luster lace bracelets.

In Menominee, where my family resided, there were four Catholic Churches and three schools all within five blocks. If you were French you went to St. Anne, the Irish attended St. John's, and the Germans, Epiphany. The Polish church, St. Adelbert had no school so their children attended one of the others or perhaps a public school in their neighborhood. In ninth grade we transferred to either Menominee High or to Our Lady of Lourdes in Marinette. Some parents did not want to pay the $15 tuition and public busing costs for the parochial school and it was heartbreaking when good friends made different choices.

The smell of burning leaves still haunts me, as does the vision of spray crashing over the breakwater. We hurried to watch the flashing lights of the fishermen as they swarmed to the dam with nets for the annual spring smelt run. I recall skimming across the waves of Green Bay in fourteen-foot sailboats piloted by young boys, often Sea Scouts, only too eager to give us a ride. Music, dancing, peasant dresses and crinoline skirts were all part of weekends in the twin cities.

"Where the heck did you go, Oconto?" Dad would shout after noting the 30 or more miles I had put on the odometer. In reality we just circled the loop, ran the 5th Street thrill, a tummy tickling bump on the corner of 5th Street and Carney Boulevard, drove past the houses of our latest crush and often made a swoop around Henes Park to see whose cars might be tucked into dark corners. Sometimes we even walked the mile around the park banging on fenders and screaming, "Up for air," a clever maneuver designed to strike terror into the hearts of the lovers. School picnics and birthday parties were held at the park where we ate sloppy joes, roasted hot dogs and polished them off with s'mores. We spent hours singing and swinging on two, large, wooden, double seated swings which held all of us if you were good friends and didn't mind being close.

We baby sat to earn money and pajama parties were big. I remember our loud gang of girls walking down Pierce Avenue to a sleep over at Marietta's one Friday night after screaming through a 3-D version of "The Creature from the Black Lagoon". In summer the Fox Theater held talent shows at intermission and we all supported Mary Fran as she got up to sing, "Somewhere over the Rainbow." How brave she was!

Upon graduation we went our separate ways but the lure of the twin cities did not fade. We returned, first on college breaks, and then with husbands and children in tow for weddings, class reunions and of course, Christmas. In 1991 my first grandson, one month old, made the trip to Menominee from his home in Illinois for Christmas day. In 1995 Mom died and shortly after my brother Bob and his family moved to Maryland. I remember all too well the first Christmas we stayed in Green Bay. I felt a sense of loss and the song. "I'll be Home for Christmas" brought tears to my eyes. Sometimes it still does.

The towns are still there but the populations have declined. The downtown "historic districts" are a little worn, but in summer the marina is jammed with power and sailboats. The docks are humming with people bent on making the most of vacation days. The M&M game is still played but the chain of wins and loses is no longer as significant except perhaps to those on the field. The beaches are there but few people swim and Paul Anka no longer echoes from the speakers Mr. Radick installed on the beach house. I go back for class luncheons at Schloegels or The Brother's Three and the sight of the band shell surrounded by trees dressed in fall shades never fails to bring back those carefree days of bicycle broncos, Friday night lights, Fifth Street thrills and Mrs. Paitl's hot dish.

Band Shell at Menominee Marina

Mrs. Paitl's Hot Dish
Brown 1 ½ lbs of ground chuck
Add: ½ cup finely chopped onions
½ cup finely chopped green pepper
1 cup diced celery
    Add: 14 oz. can of corn niblets 1 can cream of chicken soup; one can cream of mushroom soup; 1 large can of stewed tomatoes Boil one package of wide noodles and add to above mixture in large baking dish. Bake at 350 degrees for about 1 hour or until hot.

A DAY THAT LIVES IN MY MEMORY

"Grandma, do you remember World War II?" asked Jacob, my eleven-year-old grandson.

Most of what I remember comes from movies, books and stories but even though I was three when the United States entered the war, I remember Pearl Harbor day.

In my mind December 7, 1941, was grey and damp. Maybe that's not accurate but it fits with the time of the year and the events that occurred. My father was taking care of me while my mom, Aunt Mae and their bowling teammates spent a weekend at King's Gateway, a luxurious resort buried deep in Wisconsin's north woods. My father received a phone call sometime around noon.

Dad was an accountant and assistant office manager of Lloyd Manufacturing Company in Menominee. The call he received resulted in my being bundled into the car and driven to its North State Street factory and office facility. Lloyds is still a recognized supplier of outdoor furniture, but in 1941 they also made school desks. I learned later that they had contracted with the government to supply airplane parts as we drew closer to entering the fray in Europe, and that was probably the reason for the call from the boss. For me it was an opportunity to run around the deserted office hiding behind wooden desks and occasionally pushing a key on one of the huge black and gold typewriters. When you are three everything is large and imposing. Obviously I don't remember conversations but the fact that I remember anything tells me it was important and emotional for my father.

As in any time of crises we are eager to gather loved ones close in the safety of our homes and I am sure that that was on the minds and reflected in the faces of the men who gathered, children in tow, to welcome home the busload of wives and mothers. They were quiet in contrast to the group of somewhat boisterous bowlers who trouped off the bus eager to tell of their weekend experiences.

"We didn't know," they cried after hearing the sobering story of the attack. "The driver said that the Japanese bombed Pearl Harbor, but we didn't know it belonged to us!"

I ask you to keep in mind that these were the days before CNN, cell phones, Google or Twitter. Embarrassed by the fact that they had sung happily all the way home, the women headed for their cars as the news and implications set in.

We had air raid drills in Menominee. Lying on the floor in the living room, at the foot of the sofa, I tried to peek around curtains as the siren wailed from the roof of Washington school across the street. Did we hear planes approaching the rather remote and unlikely target in Michigan's Upper Peninsula? It was a game for children and had I been in school I am sure I would have heard, and concocted stories, to go with the blackouts.

This is my first significant memory, only a few cloudy recollections from a 24-hour period, but the "Day of Infamy," as President Roosevelt would call it as he declared war on Japan, lives on in my mind. You can bet it will contrast sharply with the frightening memories and experiences Jacob's other grandmother can relate. She, on the same day, was a fifteen-year-old living in the place of her birth, Shimonoseki, Japan.

St. John the Baptist School: Eight Years in Four Rooms

I just read the itinerary from my granddaughter Sydney's eighth grade trip. They flew from California to visit Washington D.C., Mount Vernon, Gettysburg and New York. When I was in eighth grade parents drove us to visit a convent in Manitowoc, Wisconsin. It was a big deal for our teachers at St. John grade school in Menominee. The four Franciscan Sisters of Christian Charity were excited to show off their home hoping, of course, that one or more of us would discover we had a vocation. In our grade school the boys were encouraged to become priests and the girls could be a nun, or maybe a martyr.

When my kids were in grade school they hoped to be chosen as a crossing guard. In our school we tried to be the first one out the door at recess, or noon hour, so we could haul out the "horses" to block off Catherine Street, keeping the cars off our playground.

Sr. Hermangild taught first and second grades in the mid forties. She found creative ways to teach phonics. "Mother Superior" came one afternoon to listen to us recite vowel and consonant sounds using examples of the words they represented. I was assigned to do the E's and had them down pat. "A" didn't show up after lunch and I got switched. Talk about pressure!

One of our class plays involved students making and wearing bright red boxes with the letters of the alphabet. I wanted to be a box but Sister liked the way my mother set my hair in rags to produce sausage curls and to my dismay she cast me as the "fairy queen" in an alternate play.

I entered first grade in September of 1944. I marched several blocks down Dunlap Avenue to St. John's grade school with Peggy Paitl, Nancy and Joey Benesh and Peggy Madden. Interestingly, we all lived on the same block as St. Anne's but we were Irish and the French went to St. Anne.

I was a honeybee because I was born ten days too late to attend kindergarten at Washington Public School the year before. Mary St. Peter tells me that when I entered the room she said, "She didn't go to kindergarten." Talk about a pariah! But Mother taught me to read while they were cutting and pasting.

Sister Hermangild and her first and second graders

In third grade we moved upstairs where Sr. Romanus, the Principal, taught third and fourth grade. She was a kind and capable instructor but my most vivid memory is the day she stood on the front steps at noon hour and with a big smile on her face, beckoned to me. She pointed to the picture I had colored and brought to school that morning and said, "Tell your mother ducks have two legs." Mother had drawn four. In later years she received more than one anonymous newspaper article with a picture of a malformed duck.

Along with a small library, the second floor also contained the fifth and sixth grade classroom. Sister Adele, a demanding woman, was our teacher those two years. I liked it when she introduced us to art by having us color reproduced pictures of famous paintings. Millet's, *The Angelus*, covered both art and religion. She also believed that memorizing poetry helped to develop minds and I can still recite some of Masefield's Sea Fever. "I must go down to the sea again, the lonely sea and the sky, and all I ask is a tall ship and a star to steer her by." I was told years later that she had been abused as a child and eventually suffered a breakdown. How sad for a woman who devoted her life to teaching children.

I bristle when I hear nasty nun stories because, while I know some wielded rulers as weapons, I did not experience that and have been forever grateful to the Franciscans and Notre Dames who taught me for sixteen years. I was not happy, however, when the principal made me ride Carol Dewane home on the back of my bike after I accidentally hit her in the head with a baseball bat.

Finally back on the first floor we entered junior high with Sister Paulette. These were fun years. The Menominee School System was progressive. They bused the farm kids to parochial school long before other districts and we walked along the alley next to Walton Blesch Stadium applying lipstick, without mirrors, to attend Home Economics and Art Classes. One semester Marcia Scanlon and I were asked to join Mary Lee Therriault and Joanne Provancher from St. Anne in one of the public school sections of sewing. We supported Joanne when she had to take Mary Lee to the nurse on the first day we used machines. She ran the needle through her finger.

There were only five boys in our class at St. John's so the football players walking the halls of the high school looked pretty interesting.

Mary Fran decided that she was mad about one of them and got up her nerve to pass a note to his steady, Carol, as she passed her in the hall. It read, "Get out of town!" When Loren injured his arm at practice one day, his doctor, Mary Fran's father, purposely asked him to come to the house instead of the office. Mary Fran was surprised to find him sitting in their living room. We humorously celebrated his Columbus Day birthday for years.

Long before Michelle Obama initiated her "Let's Move" program, we had our own. We spent hours playing football or baseball, whichever was in season. We jumped rope and never tired of roller-skating. On special church days, designated to save souls, we skated from to church to church. We would remove our skates, run in and say 6 Our Fathers, 6 Hail Mary's and 6 Glory Be's, run out, attach the skates to our shoes with keys and go on to the next. Who knows how many souls we sent soaring from Purgatory to Heaven! We played many facets of jacks like "Eggs in the basket "or "Over the moon", until Helen Converse got a bloody nose. That usually broke up the game.

Once a week we would march across the playground and down the sidewalk between the church and rectory to attend Mass said, first by Father Corcoran and eventually by Monsignor Holland. The Schumacher, Converse and Haasch families lived within a block and were emergency centers for band aides, phone calls and unexpected periods. Sometimes Mrs. Converse even explained a few facts of life.

Yesterday was Easter Sunday and it brought back the best memories. On Good Friday we climbed the winding staircase to the church choir loft and tried to stay alert and not giggle for Tre Ore, three hours of prayer, song and incense. One Holy Thursday Mary Fran's cat got in the door and crept beneath the pews half way to the front of church, collar bell jingling until she located us. Mary Fran had to leave to take her home.

I decided not to become a nun and no occasion has presented itself during which I could choose martyrdom. Instead I taught and counseled students and adults for 41 years. I look back and say I made it through those years with humor and determination that I learned from my eight years in those four rooms in St. John the Baptist School in Menominee, Michigan.

The Wedding of the Year

Fritz, Peggy and Mr. Bergman Ted Wolfe and Barbara Evans

W e had been planning for months. It was to be the wedding of the year, at least as far as our family was concerned. Uncle Fritz, Fred Meissner Jr., was marrying Margaret (Peggy) Bergman in Grosse Point Shores, Michigan, on July 23, 1949. Everyone was busy planning the route and the car arrangements but my main interest, at eleven years of age, was "who is going to be in the wedding?" and "what would I wear?"

I was excited because Fritz was my youngest uncle and I enjoyed hanging out with him, washing his green coupe and flying model airplanes in the field behind Signal Electric. He wrote to me from Guam while he served in the army. Once he sent me a picture of Frank Sinatra, the present heartthrop crooner and asked if I was one of the swooning girls in a Life magazine picture. I was embarrassed at the thought.

Peggy was a talented singer and an artist. She and her sisters sang together as they traveled with the USO. When we got a call that they were preforming we would huddle in front of the RCA radio trying to hear the faint station that carried their performance.

Details got ironed out and it was decided that my cousin, Barbara Evans, would be a bridesmaid and her fiance, Ted Wolfe, would usher. She, along with Peggy's sisters would wear white dresses on which Peggy would paint a spray of flowers. My mom bought me an orange sundress trimmed with white lace that was styled off of one shoulder. It was wonderfully sophisticated for an eleven year old and was perfect for the black-haired brownie I turned into each July.

Finally the weekend arrived and we set off in a caravan for St. Ignace, Michigan, where we would board the ferry to cross the Mackinac Straits. Our car was packed with Mom, Dad, my five year old brother, Bob, Barb and Ted. I was thrilled to have them ride with us because they were young and lots of fun. The other car held Barb's parents, Aunt Mae and Uncle Frank, Grandma and Grandpa and the driver, Uncle Archie. His wife, Aunt Theresa elected to stay home with their four sons, a subject of discussion among the adults.

We stayed the first night in St. Ignace across from the ferry docks. It was great entertainment to watch the boats unload and load as this was the only means of making the trip across the straits before "Big Mac" was built. In the mornng we loaded the cars with a growing sense of excitement of what was to come. My dad was an entertaining travel companion and Bob and I were separated to prevent spats.

Our headquarters was the Whittier, a large luxury hotel ten minutes from downtown Detroit built back in the days when Detroit was thriving. When not there, we were at the lovely Bergman home with its spacious green lawn rolling down to the shores of Lake St. Claire. We peered through a high metal fence, thick with foliage, trying unsuccessfully to catch a glimpse of Henry Ford Jr. who lived next door. Barb and Ted swam in the lake much to the dismay of the natives who said it was a polluted waterway.

On Friday night, some of the ladies, me included, stood in awe as Peggy had her picture taken standing in her wedding dress on the landing of an elegant staircase.

The wedding was held at a large cathedral and brunch followed at a bright, sunny resturant. The rest of the day was spent back at the house where the kids ran around on the expansive lawn and threw rocks and stones into the lake as boats and ships passed by on their way from Lake Huron to Lake Erie. In late afternoon the bride and groom rushed out and drove off amid shouts and cheers, the green coupe decorated with a string of old shoes and tin cans. As we left for our hotel we found the decoration hanging from a mailbox where the endless driveway entered the street. Eventually all fairy tale weddings come to an end and the Meissners slept one more night at the Whittier before most of them headed for home. My mother, brother and I would continue on East to visit with relatives in Pennsylvania and New Jersey. But that is another story.

Barbara   Mary Lynn   Mom   Aunt Mae

The Rest of the Story

On Sunday morning, the day following Uncle Fritz and Aunt Peggy's wedding in Grosse Point Shores, MI, family members packed for their return to Menominee while Dad drove Mother, Bob and me to the train station in Detroit. Far from ending our trip, we were about to start a new adventure visiting Mom's remaining family members. Our first stop would be Scranton, PA, where her mother's sister, Mayme Young, worked as a housekeeper for Mr. Renner, a retired and handicapped gentleman. This meant spending one night on the train and Bob and I were banished to a berth while Mom stayed up to visit with another woman traveling alone. They decided to try to catch sight of Niagara Falls as we passed by. We were a bit envious and my brother spent most of the evening sticking his head out of the curtain looking for her. I was sure he would fall from the top bunk. They never saw the falls.

My recollections of the visit are spotty but I know that there was an old-fashioned toaster that produced burned toast that we fed to birds in a large backyard garden. At the same time each day, Aunt Mayme would whistle distinctively and flocks would appear. We were constantly reminded to be quiet so as not to upset the elderly gentleman. Standing on the couch pulling the chains to the limit on his huge chiming clock was not part of the plan. A shopping trip and tour of downtown Scranton resulted in my leaving my wallet on the city bus. Mother called and confirmed that it was at the bus garage and then sent me, eleven, alone in a strange town, to recover it. I was sure I would never see them again.

Leaving Scranton after a week, we headed for Patterson, N.J., where a cousin, Lillian Schoeffel, lived with her family. They owned a jewelry store and resided in a large home, situated on a farm, in the middle of a subdivision. I still have my Grandmother's watch, engraved with a coal mine, and a cameo pin that came from Charles' store. Lillian's daughter was a high school student and she was asked to take me to the neighborhood pool. The goal of the big kids in the pool was to dive down and touch the drain below the diving board. I did not reach that goal. Years later you would hear of people drowning after being caught in the suction of a drain. Six-year-old Bob stayed behind, thrilled to watch and ride on the tractors and farm equipment harvesting the crops.

At this point Dad called. Never one to happily prepare his own meals, he was ready to spring for a plane trip home. In 1949 that was not a usual method of travel for most people and while it would have been exciting we voted no and headed for New York City. Boarding a ferry, we crossed the river to Manhattan and jumped on a tour bus at the harbor. The first site we encountered was the Queen Elizabeth docked and awaiting passengers for its return trip to England. Looking up out of the bus window it was impossible to see the top.

We walked down 5th Avenue, stopped in a variety store to buy Mother's favorite type of potato peeler and then had lunch in a automat on Wall Street. When we had chosen the food we each wanted and stood before the cashier she asked how much we owed. Unknown to us, we were supposed to keep track of the prices of the items as we selected them. Maybe the Wall Street brokers were adept at that but poor mother, even on the return trip around the deli, had a hard time.

Our last stop was a temple in China Town and then we headed for Grand Central Station where we boarded the Commodore Vanderbilt, a beautiful bullet train, on which we had booked a compartment with its own tiny bathroom. Walking through the train to get to the dining car with its sparkling china, white linen napkins, and elegant silver serving pieces, was a bit scary but with the help of friendly porters we made it for dinner. At bedtime, lying in an upper berth, I watched out the window for traces of city lights as we sped toward Chicago.

With two more legs to go, Mother decided she was running short of cash. My brother, a bit precocious, loved the French toast and hot chocolate they served so I was left behind for the final meal. When we arrived at the station in Chicago, Mother headed for Western Union. She had no credit card, nor other form of ID. Fortunately the woman in the office in Menominee knew her and clued the Chicago clerk to ask for her maiden name. "Metzger" did the trick and I could eat again.

In Milwaukee we boarded the familiar, yellow, Chicago Northwestern 400 that took us through Wisconsin and just across the boarder into Michigan. We were glad to be home and now Dad could also eat again.

The Skaters Waltzed

A crisp fall breeze was blowing stray leaves about the streets and early risers spotted evidence of frost. It was a refreshing change from the humid summer when the foghorn at the lighthouse had often sounded its eerie warning to boaters on Green Bay.

"Mom, do you know what I want for my birthday?" I asked as I eagerly anticipated the November 10 date that often coincided with the first snowfall in Menominee.

"What is it this week?" she sighed as she ironed one of the seven white dress shirts my father wore to work each week.

"Ice skates," I replied as I watched for the first white flake to fall.

"It will be awhile before they can flood the rinks and you have perfectly good skates."

"But they aren't figure skates!" I whined. Everyone had figure skates now! We had all read about Sonia Henie who skated in the Olympics and starred in movies. We had watched her in the newsreels that preceded the main features at the Lloyd Theater.

It was important that you have the right gear for the skating rink, as it was the center of social life once winter set in. A knitted angora hat and figure skates were musts once you hit eighth grade. At first we utilized the rink on Ogden Avenue in Menominee. It had a warming shack with a stove that would singe your mittens if you got too close and it was across the street from a popular yellow restaurant called, "Eat it up Diner" with a pinball machine that usually read, "Tilt". Marinette's

Higley Field would come later when we could drive or hitch a ride with someone to watch our friend Judi Olson skate. Right before one of their shows, her partner dropped her on her head and she got a concussion. Their part in the show was cancelled.

Life at the rink was always entertaining. On a good night a really cute guy, maybe Billy Rudd, might ask to lace and tie your skates for you. Sometimes you returned to the shack to have them tightened. Billy was a neighborhood boy best know for his ability to span his waist with his hands.

Then there were the skate dances and everyone waited to see whom Skippy Landry would choose as his partner. You had to be able to do a flying turn at the appropriate time as he spun you around. It was also interesting to watch the high school kids. It was big news when Cynthia Perry skated with two guys, her old boyfriend and her latest. Would that be us someday?

Each year the Menominee Chamber of Commerce held a special weekend event and crowned a Miss Menominee at the rink. The contestants skated back and forth and the judges made their choice. Then the mayor crowned the winner. The following week we recreated this experience. Unable to face rejection by my peers, I volunteered to be the mayor. Low and behold, Bill Rudd chose me. Guess he didn't know the mayor was ineligible.

Sometimes we skated at Hoefgen's house on the bay. The ice was pretty rough but the hot chocolate and treats that Lillian and Mary Ann's mom served made up for that. In college we played tag and raced about on the duck pond in Henes Park warming our frozen toes at the Gateway Café afterward.

I was not good enough to be a partner for Skippy Landry but I did have a couple of tricks that I could teach my kids when we went to the rink in Green Bay. They were impressed.

I finally took the skates down from the attic and donated them, afraid that if I took the grandkids they would have to call a rescue squad.

I have fond memories of that time and once in awhile I even wonder if Billy Rudd can still span his waist with his hands.

Our Lady of Lourdes High School

WE WERE THE SHAMROCKS: THOSE HIGH SCHOOL YEARS

The first day of high school I missed the bus. I waited a half hour for the next one and transferred to the "loop" bus that would take me from Menominee, Michigan, to Our Lady of Lourdes High School in Marinette, Wisconsin. I walked into church with no idea where to sit and sidled into a pew just as Father was starting the consecration of the Mass. Surrounded by unfamiliar faces, I felt a tap on my shoulder. A woman, dressed in Notre Dame nun garb, wide, white wimple and a wing-like, starched veil appeared at my side and hissed, "What is your homeroom?" "203," I stammered and she moved me to the other side of the church where smirking faces welcomed me.

I shudder when I recall my first day attire, a glen plaid suit and nylons—more forty than fourteen. When we changed to blue uniform jumpers and Bobbie Brooks white blouses the second week, we were required to wear nylons under our white socks and saddle shoes. Sister Francis Borgia stood at the door as we exited homeroom checking closely to see that we met the requirement, sometimes resorting to pinching an especially sheer leg. Many of the boys offered to relieve her of that duty and by sophomore year the nylons were gone.

There were entertaining moments most days. A crowded third floor study hall was monitored by Sr. Hortense who was not trained to deal with the machinations of ninth grade boys twanging bobby pins, shooting spit balls and rocking their feet so that the floor moved and the room itself seemed in danger of collapsing.

A hot lunch program was offered in the basement of the church. There we compared notes on Sister Marion's algebra teaching methods. Three rows of double desks were labeled A, B and C and a quiz and daily performance determined our seating. Fortunately I was often placed next to a math guardian angel, like Vince Bujonowski or Tim Hollihan, who figured out which problem I would get and whispered the answer to me before Sister, racing up and down the aisles with veil flying, got to me.

There were no lay teachers to teach us Religion, Science, English, Math and Latin. There were only the nuns and an occasional associate pastor of Lourdes Parish.

In tenth grade Sister Hortense, who had still not mastered the art of student discipline, introduced us to Shakespeare. I loved it and she often let me read the best roles in Julius Caesar like Portia and Calpurnia. One day she left the room for a moment and returned to find the desks turned and her class facing the back of the room.

Freshman girls usually poured punch at the prom but sophomore year we looked forward to dates and new formals. Strapless net dresses with hoops and crinolines were the fashion of the day but at our school they were considered "occasions of sin". After finding the perfect dress we were required to make little satin cover ups of matching material. To assure that the proper standard of modesty was met, we then gathered at the convent two weeks before the dance to model our creations for the nuns who sat around in straight chairs taking notes. As annoying as it was for us, I now believe it was a great night for those women who eagerly awaited the fashion show. Junior and senior years, our dates waited outside to see if we "passed". We were often told to "add a little lace to that shoulder". My friend Marietta was told to stick a rose in her décolletage, as if no one would look there!

My first prom was not a success. Sister Camile whispered to me, while passing my desk in Biology, that "a nice young man" was going to invite me and I must say yes! I was hoping to capture the heart of the guy who sat behind me in study hall and I had been writing poems about the Milwaukee Braves to impress him with my interest in sports. The only one impressed was my dad who sent them to a sports writer at the Milwaukee Sentinel. He wasn't impressed either. My dream date took someone else to the prom and the nice young man, who had been following me around since second grade, trapped me in the girl's bathroom. I sat on the floor crying and when the bell rang for Sister De Pazzi's geometry class, I had to come out. In those days it was thought that if you turned one person down no one else would ask you, so I said yes. We double dated with another "nice young man" who would be my date for dances for several years to come.

Easter break was early that year. Sitting in English class on a lovely spring morning, my wandering attention suddenly focused on the permeating odor of smoke drifting in open windows. Soon sirens were blaring and we were dismissed as firefighters fought a damaging blaze in Lourdes church. Sadly, parishioners had to find a different church to worship in that Holy Week and for weeks to come.

Summer days were spent at Victory Beach in downtown Menominee. We sat in our favorite spot and gathered our towels around an orange and white portable radio operating on a very large, expensive battery. The local DJ took requests each afternoon and we waited eagerly hoping that someone would dedicate a song to us, maybe <u>Hey There</u> or <u>You, You, You</u> ...anything before the battery died!

Our only gym had been a little box on the first floor but in our junior year an addition was completed holding a new facility, which also served as the "Shamrock Roller Rink". Father Fredricks was in charge and he ruled with an iron hand...and a loud microphone.

The summer of '55 found some of us with part time jobs. I worked for Bouche's Bungalow Bakery in the Krambo Food Store. Each Friday, just before nine, I helped pack up the unsold goods, dabbed on my favorite perfume, Coty's Emeraude, and headed for the Armory to the local teen dance. I may have been invited to dance more if I had just continued to smell like a donut.

Outfitted in our old navy uniforms and white bucks, sporting our new, gold, Josten rings, we began senior year. We posed for pictures taken by Ed Woleske or Baker's Studio and Sister Mary Daniel was our homeroom and first period English teacher. Each noon hour "Big Dan" would lock the door and go to lunch. Returning she would find us sitting in the room listening to Dick John strumming rubber bands on a ruler and singing "Blue Suede Shoes".

On December 2, 1955, we attended a basketball game in Stephenson, a powerhouse among Michigan schools. They were beating us handily and boredom set in as we realized the futility of such cheers as, " Our team is red hot!" After a string of calls against us we began to yell, "The ref beats his wife!" The technical foul we received added another point to make the final score 110-44. On February 7, 1956, the Stephenson Eagles, led by the top prep player in Michigan, Mel Peterson, traveled to the Lourdes gym and justice was served as the Shamrocks came out on top 68-66. The next morning we made a few victory laps around the gym, shouted a few cheers for the team, and were sent home. We were given the day off...because we won a basketball game! People talked about our win and Peterson's 41 points for years.

The theme of senior prom was "Summertime" and Mr. Harold Zahorik began the long-term tradition of the Windsor Players by staging the school's first senior class play, <u>The Little Dog Laughed.</u>

Those last days went by fast. While some were taking college placement exams, others were enlisting to serve their country and Judy and Linda excitedly planned weddings.

On June 3, 1956, fifty-one seniors received diplomas from Father Leo Courtney. On that last night I did not miss a bus and I knew exactly where to sit....between Theresa Mayer and Rosetta Miller.

This is what I recall although others have different memories. My Lourdes friends are my oldest and dearest and I eagerly look forward to luncheons and reunions to hear how they remember those high school years.

Jr. Prom in 1955 in turtle neck formals.

From Lake Fanny Hooe to the Atlantic: Get Your Kicks on Highway 41

My father's philosophy of travel was, "see your own state first," so we made many short excursions through Michigan's Upper Peninsula. We boarded a raft and pulled on ropes to cross Kitchitikipi, as we observed the "big springs" bubbling up from below. We traveled on a covered boat to see Tahquamenon Falls. In 1950 when the Korean War was declared we sat and watched huge freighters make their way through the locks at Sault St. Marie and heard on the way home that they had been closed for security reasons. We ferried back and forth across the Straits of Mackinaw from St. Ignace to Lower Michigan and much later drove Big Mac.

In 1955, we spent several days on the Kewanau Peninsula. As we stood in Fort Wilkins Park at Copper Harbor, overlooking Lake Fannie Hooe, we were surprised to hear Dad announce, "Someday we will drive to the other end of Highway 41". I'm not sure whether my brother Bob or I realized at that moment that it ended in the state of Florida and as a high school junior with a steady boyfriend and an active gang of girl friends I doubt that I was eager.

However, one year later, my father's business closed for a month and two days after my high school graduation, Mom, Dad, Bob, who was twelve and two days old, and I packed the cooler with ham sandwiches on fresh bakery rolls and cold bottles of Coke and set out for Miami, Florida.

Never an early starter, Dad always drove until dark and then we frantically searched for vacancy signs on motels and talked our way into restaurants locking their doors for the day. That first night, in Terra Haute, Indiana, we fell upon our first taste of the South, deliciously fried chicken and hot buttered biscuits with gravy. We would eventually sample grits with our morning breakfasts.

Not far into day two of travel we began to spot "See Rock City" signs on every barn and birdhouse. Unable to resist the call we headed up Lookout Mountain, near Chattanooga, Tennessee, where on a clear day you could see seven states and two civil war battlefields. Massive rock formations, believed to be 200 million years old, are set amidst hundreds of wildflowers, plants and trees. Brother Bob, searching for a drink of water, was snatched away from a "black" drinking fountain. That night we stopped, before dark, in Adairsville, Georgia, as the scheduled appearance of Elvis Presley on the Milton Berle show was a must see for me. Promising to show him only from the waist up, lest his gyrations negatively influence thousands of teen worshipers, the program made history. We watched a snowy picture on a tiny black and white TV.

Having had my driver's license for only a year, my father was determined to give me experience on the road and turned over the wheel in Atlanta, Georgia. One of my mother's goals was to ride down Peachtree Street made famous in the movie <u>Gone with the Wind,</u> but unfortunately I could not find it....and my dad did not try. This was a bone of contention for years until mother discovered that there are five Peach Tree Streets in Atlanta and no one was ever sure which one Scarlet and Rhett used to escape through walls of fire.

On Thursday, June 7, we pulled into Orlando, Florida, and located the home and general store owned by previous Menominee residents, Jesse and Cal Sweihart. Good friends and loyal patrons of Meissner's Bar, they welcomed us, eager to show off their new location and to hear news from home.

Walt Disney had recently opened his Disneyland Theme Park in Anaheim but Disneyworld was a long way off as we headed to Cypress

Gardens. It was a warm, sunny day and we lunched outside while watching beautifully costumed water skiers and when it ended we headed for Venice, Fl. We were unable to practice the water skills we had witnessed because when we checked out the motel pool we discovered a baby alligator abandoned by its former owner. Unfortunately selling souvenir alligators was a business in the South.

The next morning we drove to Naples, and stopped to visit Helen and Bill Harter. With Menominee connections they came each summer to stay at a cottage on M35 and one of their two daughters, Hillary, had become a friend of mine.

Driving south once again we approached the Sunshine Skyline Bridge. More experience for me Dad decided so I jumped into the driver's seat and set out across the four-mile span, an awesome and somewhat intimidating trip across a section of the Gulf of Mexico from St. Petersburg to Terra Ceia. In 1980 it was partially destroyed when a large ship hit one of the bridge spans on a blustery day. I can still hardly bear to think about the terror that those people experienced as they drove through the fog, off the end of the bridge into the dark, churning water below.

We explored Sunken Gardens in St. Petersburg, and then wound our way along the Tamiami Trail, the last 264 miles of US 41 stretching from Tampa to Miami. Watching to see gators and other creatures we were surprised to observe women and children washing clothes by pounding them on rocks in the swamp along the side of the highway.

Arriving in Miami Beach on June 9, we drove past the famed Fontainebleau Hotel where many celebrities stayed and performed and then checked into our somewhat less impressive Tropicana Motel. The cockroach in the shower was dispensed with immediately and was really the only creature we encountered with the exception of a stag beetle confined to a jar and displayed in a gas station. The attendant would tease the beetle by inserting an eraser and then pulling it out when the beetle grabbed. Yuck!

We swam in the pool on the edge of the Atlantic and listened to the waves crash behind us. Bob, bent on diving bombing whoever was in the pool, discovered that it was filled with salt water as he licked his lips and grimaced. We walked the beach and gathered shells and pieces of debris washed up by the surf.

Leaving Miami on July 11, we made a quick stop in St. Augustine, the oldest known settlement in the state, visited Marineland and finally Africa USA. Marineland will always be my favorite theme park and my retirement gift from my children was a swim with the dolphins in California.

Africa USA, in Boca Raton, was an experience I will never forget but not because of the uniqueness of the uncaged wildlife roaming the park. Riding a tram with a group of tourists the "children" were encouraged to jump off at the entrance and have their pictures taken with a Machaka warrior posed with spear and full battle dress. Thinking he was a statue, I was visibly startled when he turned his eyes to look at the pale-faced teen posing next to him. My parents, taking a picture, thought it was one of the more humorous stories from our trip. (I later learned that the theme park was opened by John Pedersen, a native of Racine, WI, and it was an inspiration for Walt Disney.)

Dad, was a bit of a daredevil who enjoyed spinning around in cars on the frozen bay, and once insisted that I ride with him on the back of a huge motorcycle which he had probably never driven before. He, of course, took the wheel to motor down the famed "Miracle Mile" at Daytona Beach crowded with swimmers and sun seekers caught in the annoying tourist traffic. This may or may not have been the start of Bob's avid interest in car racing which he still follows closely. We stayed that night in Ormond Beach and then headed north on June 12, to Statesboro, Georgia.

By now the days were getting longer and the siblings in the back seat were getting weary of the old comic books and each other. The novelty of the devices purchased to suck juice out of fresh oranges was wearing thin although we were finding great bargains on Coke in Georgia, where it was manufactured.

On June 13, we pulled into Richmond, Virginia, and took in historic landmarks such as the Mary Washington House and then headed into the first of many trips to the nation's capital for Bob and me. I find the sign posted along the divided highway between Richmond, Virginia, and Washington D.C. so interesting. I sent the picture of it to Bob after his forced evacuation from the city on 9/11 with a note that read, "Some things never change."

The temperature as we pulled into a parking lot right in front of the Capitol was around 100 degrees and the tempers of the occupants in the back seat were rising in accordance. When Dad suggested that we continue on up to New York City we both voted "No."

We were ready to head for home, but first we went into the Capitol and sat in on a session of the House of Representatives. They pointed out the increased security because two years before four Puerto Rican Nationals had opened fire in the house during a vote on immigration policy. (As I said, some things never change) Thirty shots were fired and one of the five injured representatives was Alvin Bentley from Michigan who was shot in the chest. Even then the security was very minor compared to any building in Washington today. Little did we realize as we sat listening to the speakers that nearly 40 years later Bob would return to write words spoken by Representative Bart Stupak from Michigan.

Sightseeing time was basically over but we did stay in a motel overlooking the Antietam Battlefield in Sharpsburg, Maryland. Antietam was the bloodiest one-day battle in the history of the US. As in Gettysburg, I found that the spirits of those who died still linger to touch the hearts of visitors.

As we returned to the Midwest we stayed overnight in Nappanee, Indiana, where Dad wanted to visit a man from Menominee who was hospitalized after a serious auto accident. The man was grateful to see my parents and as they left he promised, "I will never forget you for this." And we remembered him years later when we heard on the local news that he had murdered his wife in a bar they owned on Willow Street in Green Bay. He was believed to be hiding out just north of Menominee on the Bay Shore. Dad called home to tell us to lock the doors which we did until the police reported that he had taken his life and they had found his body in the woods off of M35. He had stopped in the tavern that morning asking for Dad.

Saturday found us in Chicago and we visited the Adler Planetarium in the morning and Riverview Amusement Park in the afternoon. On the evening of June 16, we spent the night with Bill and Margaret Ritchie, long time friends of my parents. Their daughter Susan was my age and we hung out together over the years. And then, on June 17, we headed for home. The boyfriend and the girlfriends were happy to see me and I headed for the beach with my Florida tan. It was back to work in a slightly remodeled tavern for Dad, and Bob and his buddies resumed whatever sand dune adventures they were involved in. Mom began preparations to settle us into our new home on 17th Avenue and while it was good to be back in the UP we all had lingering memories of our time traveling Highway 41 from Lake Fannie Hooe to Miami Beach in the summer of '56.

Life in the Miniature Lanes

"I can't believe my friend's father owned a bowling alley!" recently exclaimed, Mary, my grade school, high school and college classmate and friend of 70 years! Well, it was just a small one, with two lanes and duckpins. There was no automatic scoring and real people endangered their lives setting pins....but it sure made life interesting. The address 2501 to 2509 13th Street tells the story of the large building housing Meissner's Bar. Besides the lanes, where leagues competed regularly on weeknights, there were two bar rooms, and a large kitchen that at one time served complete chicken and fish dinners for up to $1.75. A local barber rented space in the front of the building for a number of years.

The old building in need of paint, many years after it was sold and before the apartment and lodge room were torn down.

Above the main bar, you could find "the lodge room" where groups of men and women---the Royal Neighbors or local unions, held periodic meetings. A small kitchen supplied the occasional suppers or snacks that were included. When great-grandfather, Ferdinand, purchased The Green Bay Hotel in the late 1800's, there were also rooms to be rented. In the 50's they housed excess furniture and various family belongings that I considered treasures.

The hotel purchased by Ferdinand Meissner in 1888 later became Meissner's Garden and then Meissner's Bar.

I spent hours sitting on the floor of one of those rooms pouring over my parents' 1923 Menominee High yearbooks and my mother's <u>Girl Graduate</u>. It was filled with dance cards, play programs and ticket stubs. Years later my dad would hand her movie or game tickets and say, "Here, put this in your Girl Graduate."

Another cedar chest held the blue, two-piece knit suit she wore at their wedding in St. John's rectory in 1936, and formals from long ago dances. We used those to stage a play Marcia Scanlon and I wrote in eighth grade.

I also spent hours in the lodge room picking out notes to popular songs on a gutted player piano. The rolls were stored in a closet above the basement stairs in my grandparent's home and the piano ended up in an antique shop in the old Lloyd's building downtown with a sign that said, "...from Meissner's Bar".

Above the back bar, the one I suspect was used during prohibition when the front one was turned into a soda shop, was the three bedroom apartment that Grandpa Fred built for us when Dad bought him out in 1947. It had a laundry room and eventually held an automatic washer and dryer…rare in those days.

On summer evenings open windows allowed for the base beat of the 50's tunes to reverberate in our living room. I remember one very hot night when mother was helping Dad, my brother Bob and I entertained ourselves by tossing ice cubes out of the living room window to land in front of people walking toward the door. They squealed on us and game didn't last long.

A tradition in our grade school was for the boys to ask the girls out on the night we graduated from 8th grade. Our class consisted of 5 boys and 14 girls so I asked to have a class party in the bowling alley. The Paitls and the Scanlons offered to help with the food and Dad tripped the jukebox so the girls could dance together and everyone could bowl. A special unwired speaker carried the music to the back room…a fore-runner of WIFI?

St. John's class of 1952

Lourdes Class of 1956 (Birgetta Rynesh, Jane Hamilton,
Darrell Hebert, Mike Lindsey, Judi Olson Ted Klaver
and Diane Kuntz. (November 10, 1955)

My sweet sixteen birthday party gathered a large group of my Lourdes classmates. At this one we danced with boys and someone actually knew how to score a bowling game.

A less successful grade school party took place in the lodge room sometime during junior high. Two of my more competitive girlfriends tangled in a game of musical chairs. One of them landed on the floor when the music stopped and both ran crying to the phone to call their mothers. Mother intervened and convinced them to stay for cake and ice cream.

The backyard was no less entertaining. A large garage used for heaven knows what helped me to get to know my new high school classmates. Ray Geniesse hauled in a farm wagon (he drove in ninth grade) and we built and stored the freshman homecoming float in that building. The float was terrible but everyone who was anyone came to decorate.

Ray and Bill Van Dyke prepare to deliver the float.

A series of small, attached sheds lined the back parking lot. Grandpa stored his building supplies in some and one held our bikes and lawnmower. It was also our house when the neighbors gathered. My naughty "daughter" the youngest Swanson child would run and hide and I always had to find her.

Mary Lynn and Bob in front of the "sheds" with Nicky. He was cute but he grew up to bark and growl at customers and had to leave.

We played football in the fall and baseball in the summer. The field was perfect with the exception of a rusty garbage burner that had to be avoided on long passes or home runs.

As people often say, we left the house after breakfast and, except for meals, we came in at dusk. We were all within shouting distance of our parents. We dodged a few Jozitas beer trucks and George Gaugh the Garbage Guy checked to see who was winning as he came for his first beer of the day. In the evening we either played Hide and Go Seek, Red Light, Green Light, or Kick the Can. Sometimes we sat in the grass in old Lloyd's lawn chairs looking at stars and gabbing with customers on their way to the bar for a nightcap. One night, that I will never forget, we visited with a favorite neighbor on his way home. He was always friendly and he dressed as a clown in the city parades. Later that evening my dad received a call that he had committed suicide. I questioned everything we had heard him say for a long time afterward.

Mother and Dan next to the lanes with the lodge room upstairs.

I graduated from high school, in June of 1956, and my bowling alley parties were over but my brother, who was just 12, has more memories of his experiences in the building he remembers with great fondness. He was really upset when they tore down the upstairs rooms. My parents purchased their first "real" house, for cash, in 1956, but Dad owned the bar until 1972 when it passed from the Meissner family for the first time since 1888. Even my daughter, Lisa, has memories of her Sundays helping Grandpa clean. He would trip the jukebox and the bowling machine and after she had done her job of sorting coins, she could listen to <u>Tiny Bubbles</u>, or <u>Windy</u>.

The building has since been sold again and a huge remodeling job has taken place...just in the front. There were rumors regarding its intended use but for a year or so no further change has taken place and no action is visible on the property.

Who is that Masked Man?

"**H**enrietta, a terrible looking man just walked in the door!" cried Eunice Anderson, clasping my mother's hand.

"Oh, it's just Leonard," replied Mom without even glancing over her shoulder as she continued to discuss the church meeting they had just attended.

"No," insisted Eunice, "he is wearing a mask!"

Stopping for a quick drink and visit after the meeting, Mother and her friend arrived at Meissner's Bar just in time for comedy hour. Meissner's, a small neighborhood bar on Broadway in Menominee had been in my family for three generations. Great-grandfather Ferdinand bought it in 1888 when it was known as The Green Bay House. He was a strict, imposing-looking man who did not allow smoking or swearing. Grandpa Fred took over around 1903 and Meissner's Garden became a popular stop with twenty-five cent fish fries and seventy-five cent chicken dinners. He also hired popular dance bands like Roy DeGainer's who later advertised that they "played on Broadway." Dad wanted no part of serving food but the two miniature bowling lanes attracted nightly leagues and the Finntown followers kept coming for 10 cent beer and 35 cent mixed drinks.

This particular evening Dad had donned one of this favorite getups, a nylon stocking pulled over his head, a hat and overcoat. He walked calmly to the bar and ordered a drink. I doubt that he fooled anyone but Eunice which, I am sure, was his intention. When he knew one of my friends was coming to the house he would lie on the couch with his bathrobe over his clothes and a nylon covering his face. This never failed to produce hysterical screams and then laughter.

Occasionally Dad would slip out from behind the bar, dress in a somber outfit and re-enter through the front door. Proceeding down the bar with hat in hand he would quietly mumble something like, "Salvation Army" and without turning patrons would drop change into the hat.

On my wedding day, as I stood in the living room in my robe he appeared in his pajama top and sport coat with a flickering "tension" sign around his neck, ordering pictures to be taken. Later in the day he dressed as a street sweeper and cleaned debris from 18th street… wearing my bridal veil.

Mary Lynn and Leonard August 19, 1961

My very early memories of Dad include lying in bed on Sunday morning listening to the bells of the German church peal while he read me the comics. He was a patient man who was kind when my friends and I got busted for throwing snowballs at cars in front of our house on the busiest street in Menominee. I was four. He was less patient, and I feared a spanking, when at age 16, four of us "borrowed" my grandmother's car while she was at Bingo. It was just sitting there since Grandpa died but unfortunately we took too many swings around the loop and we returned just as my aunt and uncle were bringing her home. Fortunately they caught us and not the police because I am not sure what the penalty was for unlicensed drivers transporting "borrowed" property across the state line.

From high school graduation in 1923, until 1946 when he took over the bar, Dad worked in the accounting department at Lloyd's Manufacturing. They produced the Lloyd Loom that became famous in the manufacture of woven casual furniture that is still made today. They thrived during the depression making school furniture and later cooperated with the war effort producing airplane parts. A division of Heywood Wakefield, the home office was in Boston and when Dad became assistant office manager he traveled East with his boss. We eagerly awaited his return on the Greyhound bus that dropped him off in front of our house on Ogden Ave.

Dad was an electronics freak encouraged by the fact that his brother owned a radio electronics store in Marinette. In the early 40's we sat before a large RCA Victor radio in a beautiful wooden cabinet listening to Fibber McGee and Molly. Both parents were fond of base-ball and the Chicago Cub games were broadcast before other team owners became comfortable with the concept. Sunday afternoon car rides ended with "Who knows what evil lurks in the hearts of men? The Shadow knows."

I know we were one of the first in town to own a TV. It sat on a table in the back room of the tavern and along with a few customers we would sneak in to watch WTMJ-TV in Milwaukee broadcast snow with occasional exciting black lines running through it. Dad erected a huge antenna, set up boosters, moved one set unto a shelf in the barroom and one into our living room. Mother's friends came to watch Liberace; Bob's to see comics and the Mickey Mouse Club. In 1953, the Norbertines launched WBAY-TV in Green Bay and the era of Gillette Friday Night Fights began.

My friends also came but a large reel-to-reel tape recorder was our favorite toy. The Four Bids, our high school's cute barbershop quartet, came to record and listen to themselves in our kitchen. We also hid it behind chairs at parties and taped people who did not know who or what they were confessing to.

Dad was a kind man who cared for his customers and neighbors as he did his family. "Eddy", a regular who told stories about surviving the Peshtigo fire in 1871, would appear in the morning and then nap for a bit with his head on a table in a side room. Dad cashed his monthly check, paid his bills, took him grocery shopping and eventually drove him to the Veteran's Hospital in Milwaukee to live.

I am embarrassed that I marched to a neighbor's house and brought home my two-wheel training bike that I thought they had stolen. Dad gave away any toys in which we know longer showed an interest. We mourned the loss of my brother's Bozo the Clown record albums with follow along books. Many times we listened to Bozo Under the Sea, turning the pages to the sound of gurgling bubbles. My Sparkle Plenty doll, (Dick Tracy's child) disappeared in a similar manner.

I can't begin to count the number of funerals Dad either drove for or served as pallbearer. It seemed he was always taking the car to be washed and cleaned of dog hair.

Dad believed you should see your home state before traveling elsewhere so we often traveled the Upper Peninsula of Michigan. When he was president of the Tavern League we made stops to check on other members. My brother and I either sat in the car or if it was not busy we drank pop and played the jukebox or pinball machine…. if we were very quiet and careful.

Dad retired in April of 1971 and the bar was sold to a newcomer to Menominee, Frank Gentile. So many years of working in a smoky, alcohol-related atmosphere had taken its toll on his health. After a pleasant trip to California to visit my brother Bob and his wife, Dina, he suffered a stroke in October while playing Yahtze at his sister's house. He drove home and shortly after a massive stroke paralyzed his left side. With limited speech he informed visitors to St. Joseph Lloyd Hospital that he was playing a game and suffered a stroke of luck. Ever the comedian! Lying in bed for five months aggravated his emphysema and it caused his death in February, 1972. He was 67 years old.

My father took me for my first plane ride with a pilot he knew at Menominee County Airport, insisted I ride behind him on a giant Harley I am sure he had never driven before, and entertained us in the winter by spinning our Nash in circles on the ice on Green Bay. I loved him dearly and for a long time after I thought my heart was broken. I was thankful, however, that he died before Mother as I doubt he would have made it on his own. When she came to visit me for a few days he would call with an excuse as to why she should come home. Once he said the refrigerator needed cleaning. Mother, on the other hand, lived alone in her home till she was ninety. And that is another story!

Dad disguised as Captain of Bob's ship the Long Beach

Henrietta and Bob

How Do You Do? I'm Henriette Meissner

In 1905, the first Nickelodeon opened in Philadelphia. Albert Einstein, age 26, was working on a PhD and the New York Giants baseball team played the Chicago Cubs and the Boston Beaneaters. On August 15, 1905, Henriette Mary and Mary Margaret were born to Elizabeth and Charles Metzger in Detroit, Michigan. The tiny twins slept in their incubator, a box in front of the open oven door. Their mother would later claim that because of all the visitors, Mary Margaret died of pneumonia at five months. There is not a lot of information about the Detroit days. My mother, Henriette, spoke of an island they lived on, probably in Lake St. Claire. Children would wait on the dock for the boat bringing groceries in the morning.

In 1910, Grandpa's employer, the Globe Tube Mill moved to Milwaukee, Wisconsin, and with Grandma's brother already there, the family followed. Charles bought the Detroit Hotel, a bar and rooming house, to accommodate former co-workers. Unfortunately his partner, Mr. Harris, embezzled and just when Grandpa was getting things straightened out he suffered a fatal heart attack swimming with his children in Lake Beulah. Mother was eight. I believe the early, big-city life, provided experiences and a certain sophistication she enjoyed and retained.

The widow Metzger operated a deli that catered to Marquette University students. Mother attended St. Rose of Lima and later graduated from 8th grade at Gesu on Wisconsin Avenue. Establishing her independence at an early age she proclaimed her disinterest in learning German. When the Frauline came to her classroom she listened while the others participated and probably learned as much as they did without being held accountable. She spoke fondly of attending movies and eating dinner at Charlie Toys, 300 Wisconsin Ave, above Walgreen's. She returned there with us for many years.

In 1920, Grandma Metzger, Mother and her brother Kenneth, the surviving children of five born to Charles and Elizabeth, moved to Menominee, Michigan, when Grandma's brother, George Thust, bought a box factory for his sons. They were not interested and when the venture failed and the others left, Grandma opted to stay in the small town to raise her two children and George's daughter, Regina. All three graduated from Menominee High School. Mother stayed for 71 years.

Mother was a reader. She would curl up in the corner of the couch with one of two daily papers, a book, a crossword or often a volume of the World Book encyclopedia. She followed the news and devoured mystery stories. She taught me how to read before I entered first grade and until she died passed on titles of her favorite books from Agatha Christie's The Murder of Roger Ackeroyd, to biographies of famous people like the Kennedy's.

We played school and she drew pictures for me to color. After reading the story of a duck that had built a nest on a downtown Milwaukee Bridge, she drew a picture of Gertie that I brought to show my teacher. Sister Hermangild and the principal, Sister Romanus, beckoned to me at noon hour and laughingly pointed out that the bird had four legs. Mother admitted she had had a hard time placing the last two legs and over the years received anonymous mail with pictures of malformed ducks.

During the Christmas season, we listened to Billy the Brownie on WTMJ and when I was in 8th grade we took the Chicago Northwestern "400" to Milwaukee to shop at the Boston Store and Gimbals, eat at Toys, attend Gesu Church and watch the Santa Parade pass in front of the Plankinton Hotel.

Introduced to sports by Mother and Dad, we were taken to watch major league baseball. They sometimes attended Green Bay Packers games at Old City Stadium and we listened on the radio before TV. We lunched at Chicago's Palmer House before a Chicago Cubs game and on one trip to Milwaukee we saw Les Paul and Mary Ford and the Milwaukee Braves. We were in the crowd in front of the Milwaukee Road Depot when the Braves made their Wisconsin debut and included in a picture on the front cover of Life Magazine.

Mother saved money from her allowance to buy me good clothes and she was determined from early on that we would receive college educations. And then there was her other life.

Henriette and Leonard Meissner both graduated from Menominee High school in 1923. They hung out with the same crowd but never dated until both went to work in the office of the Lloyd Manufacturing Company. In 1936, Father Cleary married Mother, a Catholic, and Dad, of undetermined religious affiliation, in the rectory of St. John's Church. Mother was 37 and Dad 36. I was born two years later and Bob in 1944.

They hung out with a group of friends, golfed and had dinner parties, often eating at Grabby's, a steak house in Marinette. That all changed in 1947 when my grandfather decided it was time for him to retire from the bar business that his father had opened in 1888. Not ready to give up working completely he talked Dad into taking over and allowing him to "help out". The pay would certainly be better than Dad earned as head accountant and assistant office manager at Lloyd's, but for Mother it was a difficult transition. There would be fewer friends, no more card clubs and dinner parties, and she later admitted she cried herself to sleep for many nights.

She didn't spend a lot of time in the bar when we lived upstairs but she helped out on New Year's and after the M and M game….the yearly football competition between Marinette and Menominee, the oldest interstate high school football rivalry in the country. Dad told a story of two men who got into a heated discussion on one of these occasions. Mother, about 5 feet tall, planted herself between the two men and instructed them to behave as she pointed to the door. For years I looked for an opportunity to emulate her bravado.

Mother was a good cook finding a variety of ways to prepare Dad's favorite food… hamburger. Her Swiss steak with homemade noodles was the best and we would come home to find the noodles hung to dry over the backs of chairs in the kitchen. If you dared turn down something or refuse seconds she was sure you did not like it and she never forgot. If you ate it all, it was obvious to her that she had not made enough. She counted everything. I still know how many meatballs there are supposed to be in her batch of Swedish Meatballs and I count rolls or pecan fingers as I prepare them. If the number is not close, they are either too big or too small and I reroll. You must only brown 10 meatballs at a time and I feel guilty if I impatiently toss in 12. One night we sat in our little kitchen, in their first real home after 20 years of marriage, and watched with rapt attention as she made Baked Alaska to top off a meatloaf.

Mother had a hand's off method of parenting as evidenced by one extreme example. On a Sunday morning after church, I went to play on the St. Ann's school playground with my friends. I was called home to a disturbed household to hear that my baby brother had crawled through a hallway, out the front door (which I was accused of not having shut properly) across the porch, down the steps, along a 20-foot sidewalk, over the curb and into the middle of the street in front of the house. That street was Ogden Avenue and a lady driving across the Interstate Bridge stopped to pick up a squirming, white bundle in the middle of Highway 41. She knocked on our door looking for its owner.

I laugh when I recall stories from later years. She complained that Dad would come home from work in the early morning hours and slam cupboard doors. She inevitably left one or two open and he would walk into them. The idea of making sure they were closed before she went to bed did not seem to occur to her.

Mother liked TV and it was her companion from morning till late night. In early years her friend Eunice would come to watch Liberace and in later years the grandchildren had to compete with M.A.S.H. It clashed with my son's favorite Emergency and the kid didn't have a chance. She was aghast at the thought that a child would determine programming.

Mom lived alone in her home for twenty-two years after Dad died at 68. Bob or Dina took her to the library for her week's supply of reading material, to Niemann's for her groceries and to the bank for cash that she brought home and stowed in a Bible. She visited us armed with a week's supply of food that she had prepared.

In January of 1995, my husband and I traveled to Menominee in snow. My friend, Mary Staudenmaier, had invited me to do a presentation for a woman's day sponsored by her bank. That evening we trudged through more snow, to have dinner with Bob and Dina. In the morning when Gene and I got up and prepared for church I glanced in her bedroom and noticed that she was in a strange position in bed. I was devastated to discover that she had had a heart attack in the middle of the night and we never heard her if she called for help. Dina later disclosed that she had been thinking about what we would do as it appeared it was getting harder for her, at 90, to manage alone.

Mother died on the same day as Rose Kennedy, the matriarch of the famous family. Bob made me laugh through tears as he imagined mother following Rose down the line of her deceased family members waiting to welcome her. His imitation of Mother, smiling meekly, hands folded at her waist, bowing slightly and repeating, "How do you do? I'm Henriette Meissner," was perfect.

Henrietta, Leonard and Toby

GRANDPA FRED: A WINNER AND STILL CHAMPION

I sat beside my grandfather on a bench in front of the fireplace watching as he stuffed the toe of his shoe with crumpled newspaper.

What happened to your toes?" I asked, as he slipped the shoe over his toeless foot. I don't recall that he answered but I can picture his quiet smile reflecting patience with a young granddaughter's questions. Eventually I learned that he and a friend were jumping a train for a joy ride. It wasn't the first time but certainly the last as he fell and his foot slipped beneath the metal wheels of the freight car.

The family remembers Grandpa Meissner as gentle man, slight, with grey hair and wire rim glasses. His obituary, however, written in February of 1953, describes him as "a chap who was pretty good with his dukes in the rough and tough lumberjack days at the turn of the century."

The paper says that Fred Meissner, christened Ferdinand after his father, was born in Green Bay on November 25, 1876. I was always told that his family lived in Francis Creek in Manitowoc County. They moved to Menominee, Michigan, when he was eight where his father operated a bar.

Ferdinand and Anna (Stauber) Meissner with sons Fred and Wilfred.

Boxing was a big sport in those days and if a participant was lucky the promoter might take in enough to pay his carfare home. Grandpa reached his peak as a fighter in the late 1800's and early 1900's. Described as a welterweight at approximately 147 pounds, he often held his own with heavier opponents because of his skill.

One particular story, written in the local paper tells of matches held in the Danish Hall on January 24, 1903. *"The fight between Fred Meissner of Finntown, lightweight champion and Kid Rogers of Detroit was expected to be a good one with heavy betting on both sides. Rogers was confident enough to place a $3.50 bet on himself before entering the ring. After exchanging a few blows, Meissner landed a stiff punch on Roger's right eye and a couple of heavy jabs to his body and he went down. Meissner stood off a short distance and then seeing Rogers raise his hand stepped in and dealt the Detroit man a hard left. There was debate as to whether his hand was really raised and the referee's decision went with Rogers whereupon he immediately arose and was declared the winner. The crowd yelled, "Fake," and piled into the ring. Meissner's manager stood on a chair offering a rematch in three weeks for $500 a side and Ferdinand, father of the loser, stood on a chair and pledged $1000 dollars if his son would be given a rematch. Neither was accepted. The crowd left in disgust and as the paper said, "It will be a hard matter to get a crowd out to another fight until Meissner is matched against someone who is known to be good and has some reputation to back him!"* (Menominee Herald Leader Jim Ripley 1/1953)

Grandpa Fred married Mina Williams in 1896 and as their family grew he took over the tavern from his father around 1903. They lived in the back of the bar building in the area that later became a popular miniature bowling alley with men's and women's leagues operating nightly. By 1905 they had five children, Wilfred, Hattie, Archie, Mae, and Leonard. Hattie did not survive her teen years and Wilfred died at 28. Their youngest son, Fred Junior, was born in 1919.

Leonard, Hattie, Mae, Archie and Wilfred.

In 1919 Michigan ratified prohibition and for one year Fred moved his business to Marinette, WI. He came back to Michigan a year later when the entire country adopted the law. The front bar became a "soda shop" but I often wondered about the "peep hole" in the back bar room door and we sometimes playfully knocked on it mumbling, "Joe sent me!"

Archie's son Richard told stories he heard of the moonshine days when farmers, who had stills hidden in county woods, would bring their product and transfer it to Grandpa's bathtub. Using the charcoal that also lined specially made hickory barrels, he further refined the home-made liquor. It was supposedly the best to be found in the area. Barrels were placed in local streams and even on ships. My cousin Paul was told that Grandpa knew the captain of the Ann Arbor car ferry who agreed to transport the barrels back and forth across Lake Michigan. The rolling of the barrels caused the color of the wood to permeate the liquor and produce a desirable color.

Another cousin, Tom, remembers Meissner's being dubbed "The Bank of Finntown" as many of the local factory workers would come on Friday to cash their checks and purchase a round or two of beverages when prohibition finally ended. The restaurant was a popular spot and the price of a chicken or fish dinner was 25-50 cents. Tom swears he rode a turtle in the big kitchen before it was boiled for soup.

Menu from Meissner's

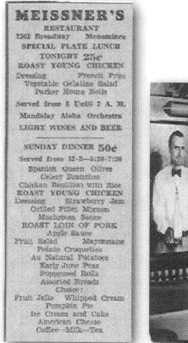

John Kubiak, Cy Quever, Fred Meissner and Charles Everard tended bar

Fred's interest in boxing never waned and he set up a gym over the tavern in what was know as Meissner's Hall where he trained and conditioned young men for the sport. My friend, Louise Jurgens Kazmer, informed me many years later that her father was one of the recipients of that training. Cousin Paul still has the original frame from the punching bag they used and he says that when Grandpa punched he could actually make the bag sing "Kansas City Here I Come!" Paul has since replaced the bag for his own workouts.

My Uncle Archie followed in his father's footsteps and his sons, Richard and Jim participated in the more organized Golden Gloves competition. When Richard boxed, his father, Grandpa and sometimes even my father, Leonard, would assist. Jim fondly recalled Grandpa attending his bouts, probably in his early seventies, and when he was introduced he leapt over the ropes to enter the ring. Jim was so proud!

My brother Bob was only nine when Grandpa died so his memories are vague but he remembers the punching bag set up in the basement of their home and called me several years ago when he discovered that his son Peter had also installed a punching bag for his workouts. He also remembers hiding in the back seat of Grandpa's Pontiac as he drove downtown to do the banking for my father who had taken over Meissner's Garden in 1947. The "surprise" as he popped up was not a popular move.

"What do you remember about Grandpa," I asked my cousin Barbara Wolfe. She and her parents lived in the Broadway home for several years. Her recollections of the quiet, gentle man resemble mine. She does not recall ever carrying on long conversations with him but she tells of the Fourth of July fireworks he arranged with a Duclan cousin, which drew the neighborhood to the empty lot behind their house. She also remembered the bench set before the fireplace and the daily shoe ritual. Her daughter Joey has the bench although it has been recovered since Grandpa's days. We both are sure that he came home for a large noon meal complete with meat, potatoes and dessert but also says they had another dinner at night when her parents returned from work.

Tom tells of Grandpa leading he and brother Jim down the basement exhibiting more than his usual exuberance. A recent purchase, a stoker for the huge coal furnace, meant he no longer had to shovel coal to heat the large home with its high ceilings and wrap around porch.

Henriette and Emma Meissner, Frank and Barbara Evans, Archie, Theresa and Richard, Tom, Fred Jr., Jim, Paul, Mary Lynn, Leonard, Mina and Fred Meissner and Mae Evans

I remember an outing to Milwaukee in June of 1949. Grandpa treated family members to tickets to a closed circuit transmission of a title match between Jersey Joe Walcott and Ezzard Charles. It took place in Chicago but the theater on Wisconsin Avenue in Milwaukee carried the bout live. It was probably not the first choice of entertainment for an eleven-year-old girl but I have never forgotten the excitement of Grandpa and other adults sharing the opportunity.

When Grandpa decided it was time to retire he asked my dad to take over the business. Giving up his job at Lloyd's was a big decision but he accepted. The move in 1947 meant Grandpa would continue to have work to do and he promised a new home for our family as he completely rebuilt a three bedroom apartment in the building complex which housed the tavern, a miniature bowling lanes, a barber shop, the upstairs "lodge room with a kitchen and boarding rooms" a large kitchen and a back bar room, a maze of property which provided continuous entertainment for my brother and me and our friends for years.

Older cousins remember the Christmases when Grandpa sat quietly at the head of the dining room table watching over his children and their families. We remember the 50th wedding anniversary celebration in June of 1946. Six grandchildren were in attendance. Four grandchildren, Susan, Mary B, Rick and Bill were not born yet and my baby brother slept upstairs.

On Thursday, February 19, 1953, my family gathered in the kitchen for our evening meal. Dad had just come upstairs from work around 6:30 to sit down at the table when the phone rang. Grandpa, on his way home from the tavern, had suffered a heart attack in his car in front of the Falk hotel a block away. His nephew, Earl Bell, had been following him and when he saw the car veer to the left and strike another car he rushed to turn off the ignition and call for assistance. While Dad hurried to the scene we peered out our window and sadly watched the flashing red lights of the emergency vehicle through the dark, damp, February gloom. Fred Meissner, the guy who was "pretty good with his dukes," had given up the fight at age 76.

GRANDMA LIVED ON BROADWAY

Fred and Mina Meissner with son Leonard. 1906

"Hey, Grandma, can I use your bathtub to call Rock Hudson?"

Okay, so I didn't really say that, but one day I did sit in my grand-mother's bathtub, fully clothed, one foot dangling daintily over the side, pretend phone clutched to my ear, picturing heaps of foaming bubbles! Think Doris Day speaking flirtatiously. I may have been in 7th grade.

Grandma liked things new. She got rid of the old, as evidenced by an authentic Tiffany lamp she replaced and stored in a box in her attic. Her bathrooms were another example. Sometime in the late 40's she had the large bathroom upstairs and a smaller powder room downstairs redone in ceramic tile. Matching fixtures complimented the lavender and green colors and they were beautiful. A family story told of a pleas-ant looking woman who came to the door asking to see the new rooms. She introduced herself, said she was redoing her house and a dealer told her that Grandma's was a showplace. Only later did Grandma find out that the woman's house was of "ill repute." She was the local madam!

Having cleaned for others in her teen years, Grandma also liked things spotless. We moved in with them for about a month in 1947 while grandpa finished our apartment. Mother and I were awakened early one morning and given dusters. It was the day the cleaning lady came and important that she would later say, "Mrs. Meissner has the cleanest house in town!"

If I am giving the impression that (Ermina) Mina Williams Meissner was frivolous or materialistic I do not mean to do so. Born in October of 1880, she married Fred Meissner when she was 17 and gave birth to eight children. One daughter, Hattie, died at 15, Catherine died at age 11 and Gertrude at 14 months. Grandma believed that Hattie contracted tuberculosis because she swam in the pool at Menominee High School in the winter. A son Wilfred died, also of TB, when he was 28. Her house was her pride and consolation.

Grandpa believed that "nothing was too good for his wife!" He was gone a lot and she cooked and cleaned and cared for the children.

When we have a family reunion or just get together with a cousin or two, Grandma's house always enters into the discussion. We all enjoyed our time there. I spent many hours on the wrap-around porch that you could enter from the front door or from the living room. It was made of wood and filled with chairs and couches. When you sat in them you could watch all of Menominee drive past on Broadway.

As you entered the house from the porch, the front parlor, or music room, was on the right and in it sat a shiny, baby grand piano. Grandma did not read music but she sat with me picking out notes of favorite songs. In the foyer, a beautiful staircase ascended to the second floor and at the foot of the stairs, on the banister, was a striking light fixture. I remember it as a lady with bronze lights in her hair. Under the staircase a deep, dark guest closet made a great hiding place for cousins' games of hide and seek.

1923 Broadway

Barbara, Susan and I all remember a special scent associated with Grandma. At a reunion last summer, Barbara and I wondered if it might have been the Coty's Emeraude perfume she always wore. We discovered, 60 years after she died, that we had both liked it and because of her, wore the fragrance introduced in the 1920's.

My brother remembers Grandma as someone who did not smile. Because I was older and spent more time with her, I recall her being an enthusiastic card player who tried to teach me Pinochle. I also saw her as a gentle woman. We once had a serious discussion about religion. Her youngest child, Fred, was about to marry his long-time love, Peggy, in the Catholic Church. He was the second son to "convert" and she confided that she would rather they change religions and attend church than not attend at all.

Barb, whose mother was the only surviving daughter, says grandma warned her, when she was in her teens, not to become boy crazy! We think perhaps because she married so young this was an important lesson for her granddaughters. Mary Beverly, born a generation after Barbara and I, only remembers Grandma wearing crocheted gloves and gently holding her hand.

Grandma cooked good food and often prepared dinner at noon. She would call my mother who sent me five blocks to pick up a bowl of sauerkraut. I would sample a few fingersful out of my bike basket on the way home.

She also prepared big holiday dinners, typical in that most kids ate in the kitchen and big people at the dining room table where Grandpa presided. She bought Christmas gifts for all of us and we sat near the brightly lit tree and stared at the ice rink made from a mirror and surrounded by cotton snow with tiny figures on skates. A large RCA radio and record player housed in a large cabinet was usually playing Christmas music and at other times, top hits that had been retired from the juke box at Meissner's Bar,

Barb remembers a room at the head of the staircase filled with hats and accessories. I remember the dressing tables with triple mirrors that again brought out the movie star in me.

From the attic to the basement, this house had something to explore and we did. Above the basement stairs was a closet that you had to be a tight ropewalker or gymnast to get to. It was filled with rolls from the player piano that sat in the meeting room above the bar. In the basement, hidden behind a curtain amidst fruit jars, was a slot machine that the adults would occasionally play and the children were forbidden to speak of.

Grandma did not drive…at least not after attempting to back the car out of the garage and instead exiting through the front wall. She did like to travel and one day called my mother to say that she was sick. Mother went to see what she could do and found her in bed complaining that Peg and Fritz had borrowed her car to run to Green Bay and did not invite her to go along. The problem was that when she did go somewhere she spent most of the time wanting to "get going" back home.

After Grandpa died she was frightened to stay alone and eventually Aunt Mae and Uncle Frank renovated the house and moved in. Grandma died of stomach cancer two years later. I was 16 and my boyfriend and I sometimes sat with her on warm summer evenings in St. Joseph Lloyd Hospital before going off to a movie. Eventually the then two-family home was sold to a church that was half the size of the house and a young minister moved in.

The house is featured often in my dreams. Barb says she wishes she could have bought it to raise her family but her husband Ted was a Marinette native and "no way were his kids going to graduate from arch-rival Menominee High!"

My cousin Tom actually stopped at the house one day and asked if he could walk through it. The owner was cooperative. By this time the wooden porch was rotted and removed and the newly tiled bathrooms were no longer Hollywood. And oh, yes, the Tiffany lamp stored in the attic because it was old? My sister-in-law was looking for a lamp to hang over her dining room table and my mother insisted that the Tiffany had never been found when the house was cleaned out. Dina and her mother went to the minister to ask if they could look for it. It was there, still in the box, in need of repair. It was too big for Bob and Dina's dining area but they suggested that the minister take it to Mary Kruez, the local antique guru. She bought it and he financed his wedding with the proceeds. Grandma would have liked that.

The Boxer and His Bride

The Menominee Flash

To me he was Uncle Archie but others knew him as "The Menominee Flash." Archie traveled to matches in Green Bay, Eau Claire, La Crosse, Milwaukee, Minnesota and Chicago as well as throughout the Upper Peninsula. He fought 100 matches, wining all but two and those he tied. He was a favorite of fans who were known to stand and cheer his work as well as his clean boxing. Unlike the days of his father's fights, contracts show that the payoff could be anywhere from $50 to $175 a bout. When Richard boxed, Archie, Grandpa and sometimes even my father, Leonard, assisted him.

My father's oldest brother became a Corporal in World War 1 and he married Thesesa Neumeier on July 6, 1921. Their first son, Joseph was stillborn but they raised four others, Richard, Paul, Tom and Jim. Sometime in the late forties I remember my mother coming to my room laughing after receiving a call from her sister-in-law. Theresa had recently had her gall bladder removed and was disturbed to find herself suffering similar symptoms. She called the Doctor to ask if the organ could have grown back. He soon showed her the evidence that the baby girl she was carrying was not another gall bladder. Susan made her appearance 14 years after her brother Jim.

In the early years, while Archie built his reputation, she had her own talent to nurture. When she was twelve, Father Schaffer, the pastor of Epiphany Church, asked her to substitute for the ailing organist. She continued in that position until 1965.

The Menominee Lloyd Theater was a popular downtown attraction where the latest films were shown. In the days before the Vitaphone was invented and synchronized dialogue was introduced, Theresa played the "Mighty Wurlitzer" organ for silent films. Sheet music was provided and the organist was required to match the up and down drama of the film. Good organists, and she was one, enjoyed improvising.

Christmas day usually meant a trip to Archie and Theresa's and the exchange of gifts with cousins. They were present at all the special moments of my life. My aunt was my sponsor and I took Theresa as my Confirmation name. On the day of my wedding, Archie drove me to church in his station wagon.

In 1936, they purchased land and a two-room cottage on M35 near Elmwood Road. Archie gradually added room after room until it became the six bedroom, 2-bathroom home my brother purchased when our uncle died. When we first visited we could ride in a rowboat from the back yard through tall sea grass to the open bay. The waves eventually wore away almost a mile of land. The night of Archie's funeral, in April of 1973, they were actually crashing on the picture windows in the kitchen and living room.

When I learned to drive in 1955, Archie and his sons were operating an electronics shop on what was called the triangle...a little piece of land across from the Fox Theater between Pierce, Vine and Wisconsin Avenues in Marinette. I would often pull up to the door or open window of the shop to say hello and Archie always seemed happy to see me. The Meissner crew was responsible for the sale and maintenance of our family and business TV's and the reason why we had one of the first televisions in Menominee... with a small screen and a very large antennae to enable us to pick up "snow" from WTMJ in Milwaukee.

In keeping with the Meissner humor, the oldest son was the quietest of the comedians. While his brother Leonard and his sister Mae donned costumes to entertain, Archie had an amusing response to most situations. This probably served him well when he acted as a bouncer for the bar that his grandfather and father operated. I can still see Theresa shaking her head, laughing at his remarks. She was not afraid to speak up and one usually knew what she was thinking.

Raising their last child in a different world was a challenge for my aunt and uncle. Susan moved to Milwaukee to attend nursing school. There she met and married Andrew during the explosive civil rights demonstrations in the city. Together the interracial couple fought for fair housing. Susan helped to form neighborhood watch programs and worked with local officials to shut down drug houses. Neither parent understood her activities at first and worried for her safety but eventually they accepted the child they had raised and taught to stand up for equality.

In the early seventies my brother sold snowmobiles for ORPI'S in Menominee. We would take them out and travel one and a half miles on the bay from Henes Park to Archie and Theresa's house. We could see the deterioration in my uncle who had been diagnosed with dementia. He smiled as we entered and appeared pleased to have visitors but he had changed from the outgoing person we knew. He didn't speak much but there were still a few jokes. My father passed away in February of 1972, and his older brother went down for the count in April of '73. Aunt Theresa died in 1999. We all knew she planned it that way. Her tombstone was already carved with that date and being a conservative lady of her day, she had to go before the millennium so it would not have to be redone! I always smile when I visit their gravesite, not far from the water in Menominee Riverside Cemetery.

Archie and Theresa

Mae and Frank

MAE AND FRANK EVANS: ASSESSING A RELATIONSHIP

"Promise me you will never cut your hair!" Those were my Grandma Metzger's dying words to me. I was six. I am not sure I would have remembered my promise or taken it seriously, even after I got it caught in the merry-go-round on St. Ann's school's playground. Mother had to come and cut me out. The next hair memory I have is sitting on a chair in my Grandma Meissner's yard, towel wrapped around my shoulders and Aunt Mae armed with a scissors. When she was through I no longer could sit on my very straight, almost black, mane.

Aunt Mae did not mess around. I don't remember my mother advising me about much as I grew into my teen years but I specifically recall Aunt Mae telling me it was time to wear deodorant. One day I was at Grandma's and there were freshly baked cookies on the cupboard. I made a casual reference to them and she said, "Don't hint. Just ask for what you want." It was a good life lesson for an awkward adolescent and I still try to follow it.

Mae Meissner Evans, born March 21, 1900, was the only surviving daughter in my father's family after three sisters died. She married Frank Evans in 1920 and they celebrated 63 years of marriage. They adopted their only child, Barbara, when Mae was 30. My husband and I adopted our son, Dan, when I was 30 and she was encouraging and shared information about their procedure and Barbara's background. I was glad to be able to talk to Aunt Mae and be assured of the happiness their daughter brought to them.

She was a hard worker. She did secretarial work for the L. E. Jones a law firm, and then worked in the office of the Superior Sugar Company. She dressed and acted the role of a professional person, but like her brother, my father, she was always up for a good laugh and willing to make herself the center of the joke.

The story I heard most often occurred at Grandma's house when friends gathered for the weekend. My parents, the Ritchies, former Menominee residents who were visiting from Neenah, my grandparents and a couple others had had drinks and a good dinner. Some were in the living room visiting while others cleaned the kitchen. Hearing a knock someone went to the door and led a woman into the room. The woman's face was swollen and smudged with dirt and she was poorly dressed. She asked for help, saying she was cold and hungry. While Margaret and others fussed trying to figure how they could help, one or two people in the group merely snickered, showing no willingness to assist. The atmosphere became tense and finally the unkind souls burst into laughter… along with the pathetic lady. Aunt Mae had slipped out, stuffed her nose with Kleenex and her cheeks with cotton, and quickly donned the outfit she had prepared ahead of time. Like her brother, who loved to put one over on the crowd, she was very successful.

Occasionally, as we sat watching TV, our phone would ring. When Aunt Mae had company she would call. When mother answered Mae would ask, "Is the wizard there?" Mother would begin reciting the numbers of a deck of cards," Ace, two, three…" When she reached the chosen card, Mae would say, "Hello, Wizard." Mother would then switch to the card suits, "Hearts, Spades, Clubs. …" Upon reaching the right suit, Mae would interrupt, "Can you tell me the card we have chosen?" and Mother would respond, "Your card is the three of Clubs." Mae's wizard friend impressed the visitors. She called one night when mother was away. I answered and she asked, "Is the wizard there?" I knew what to do, but I panicked and replied, "The wizard isn't home" and hung up. I never had the chance to redeem myself.

When I was a sophomore in high school three of my friends and I cooked up a really dumb scheme to "borrow" my grandfather's car that had been sitting in the garage since he died. We miscalculated the time and returned it just as Aunt Mae and Uncle Frank were bringing Grandma home from bingo. Of course they spotted the car parked in an alley behind the house. We ran but my glass case lying on the front seat was a significant clue. My father received a call at the same time we were calling my mother to "confess." For years Aunt Mae apologized to me for calling my dad without talking to me first. For years I reassured her that I was eternally grateful that they caught us and not the police.

Frank "Diddy" Evans was a well-know athlete, veteran and something of a politician. A winning pitcher for minor league teams (including the Twin City Packers) when he was a teen, his climb to baseball fame was interrupted when he enlisted in the Army in May of 1918. He flew to England and then on to France where he fought the German army. He and Harry Nordval started the WWI Veteran's Organization in Menominee and he was active in VFW Post 1887. He consistently campaigned for pensions and better medical benefits for all vets.

Uncle Frank began working at Lloyd Manufacturing Company and then later served for 18 years as timekeeper at Superior Sugar Company, most often referred to as the Sugar Beet. He was a great talker and when he believed in a cause he would argue his viewpoint wherever he happened to be, even on a street corner. Some people saw him as excitable. I got to see another side. I would occasionally stay with my aunt and uncle if my mother had to be away and one time stands out. It was spring and Barbara was going to attend her junior prom at Menominee High with her boyfriend Ted Wolfe, a formidable athlete from archrival Marinette High. Mae invited Mother to go with them to Green Bay to pick out a special dress for the occasion. I was to stay with Uncle Frank. He was willing to play cards or read to me but I wanted to play beauty shop. He bent over the bathroom sink and let me, a nine year old, shampoo his hair and then sat quietly in a chair, towel draped around his neck while I brushed and combed until I was sure his hairdo was perfect. He also mopped up a lot of water from the bathroom floor.

When I was a senior at Lourdes, the Catholic High School in Marinette, we had a government day and seniors could "run" for a position. In 1955, Uncle Frank was city assessor in Menominee so that is the position I ran for in Marinette --unopposed. While the tax assessor was an important job it wasn't particularly attractive to high school seniors or to the people whose property was being assessed. As we made our rounds, the Marinette assessor introduced me at each business we visited and the first question they asked me was, "Why on earth did you pick that office?" I proudly proclaimed, "Because this is what my uncle does in Menominee!" Many knew Diddy and said he was a good guy, despite his job.

Aunt Mae's health began to fail. Her memory was already fading when she experienced a bout of breast cancer. Although she had a lumpectomy, no further treatment was offered because of her age and she passed away in 1982.

Uncle Frank carried on eventually moving to the Luther Home in Marinette. We heard stories of how he made himself popular pushing people in wheel chairs to the dining room, helping other residents in any way he could. Just visiting and telling his stories cheered those who may not have had someone to talk to. He died at 87 in October of 1984, almost two years after Aunt Mae.

There are times when my brother will put on a good show but neither Barb nor I have shown a tendency to carry on tradition. She tells of the time her mother dressed her as the Hollywood vamp, Mae West. Attaching West's signature saying, "Come up and see me sometime" to

Barb's doll buggy, with family dog Rex inside, Aunt Mae sent her out to march in the Menominee Fourth of July parade. She says the grimace on her face tells exactly what the six year old thought of dressing up to entertain.

Barbara Evans and Rex

MOVING ON TO MOUNT MARY

Michigan, St. Norbert and Mount Mary College were my choices to visit on college nights. My mother chose Mount Mary, a Catholic, all women's, liberal arts school in Milwaukee. Mother grew up in Milwaukee, attended Gesu grade school, loved to visit and hang out at Charlie Toy's restaurant and wander Wisconsin Ave, but that is not why she pushed the college. Each night the announcer on the local station closed the 10 o'clock news by asking, "It is 10:30. Do you know where your children are?" If I went to Mount Mary, she could say, "Yes."

Mary St. Peter, Mary Staudenmaier and I, all from Lourdes High School were safely locked into Caroline Hall each night....literally, with chains on the doors. To further secure our safety, a nun walked around at lights out, 10:00PM, and blessed us with holy water. It was not until a reunion long after graduation that I was told some of the gals slipped her cigarettes when she passed.

When others received letters naming the roommate with whom they would share a double room, I was disappointed to learn that my room would be a single. Was there no one compatible with me? As it turned out the gal across the hall was also a Mary Lynn and next door to her was Lucero Escobar from Cali, Colombia, who spoke very little English. We sat on the floor outside our rooms and taught her useful phrases like, "Anyone for tennis?" She learned quickly that her "hall mates" were a little crazy and in self defense, she picked up the language fast. Mary Lynn Schwab decided MMC was not for her and with the help of some of the Chicago gals, I packed up her belongings and aided in her escape and elopement before second semester.

It is impossible to recreate my four years in a single memoir but there were highlights that I will always cherish. Sophomore year Mary Werth and I decided to share a room. It was an excellent decision for me. She brought me hard rolls slathered with peanut butter and jelly if I didn't make it down for breakfast and only threatened to hit me over the head with a magazine once...when I snored. Together we experienced a great moment in musical history. We turned our radios to two different stations and listened to the Everly Brothers sing "Dream" for the first time... in stereo.

This match also led to great weekend trips to Reedsburg where we climbed around on bluffs at Devil's Lake and explored a deserted Wisconsin Dells. Mr. Werth built fires in the fireplace and we cooked burgers in their living room. Mrs. Werth fussed over us and then enlisted our help in cleaning up the park across the street that her scout troop maintained.

Sharon, Monica, Mary Lynn and Judy cooking in Werth's fireplace.

Mary had a secret ambition to be a tennis player and she signed us up to play in a school tournament. We drew two more athletic classmates. Yvonne Borsch and Mary Alice Conahan laughed heartily when we confessed that we did not know how to score....but they were kind to us and happy to chalk up an easy first round win. I think Mary eventually achieved her goal and enjoyed the game.

In the fall of 1957, the Milwaukee Braves fought their way to the World Series. Each time they played at home, I sat on an open window ledge and swore I could hear the downtown crowds shouting and horns blowing. I wrote a brief poem entitled, "Oh, to be out in the world and doing things," which my roomie reminds me of every so often.

The Staudenmaiers came up with two tickets that enabled high school classmate Mary and I to watch them defeat New York! (I probably should mention at this point that being named Mary was not a prerequisite to attending Mount Mary College) We got a ride from someone who was in the office at school and heading that way. I was so afraid we would miss the Star Spangled Banner, I made Mary get out so we could run the last couple blocks to County Stadium. She was also my partner as I learned to play bridge. A math whiz, I was sure she knew every card the foursome was holding and although she never once admonished me for making a poor bid or a bad play, I was very nervous. I learned enough to make the dangerous run from the dining room down the stairs to the "smoker" each night to snag a table for four.

Junior year roommate Mary and I teamed up with Diane Tomaso and Janet Weiler and the four of us shared suites the last two years. Senior year we drew a high number and picked choice rooms on second floor... with a balcony. It was not unusual on a sunny day to have class-mates marching through our rooms in various states of undress to climb out a window and sit in the sun. Dean Celine constantly reminded us that this was not allowed and insinuated that planes flew over the school to observe the display....sure!

Suitemates Jan, Diane, Mary and Mary Lynn

Sunbathers, Helen Walker and Estelle Filipiak

We had mixers with Marquette and Janet and Diane both met their prospective husbands on the very first get together. Dan and Fred became regulars eating in our dining room on weekends when "guests" paid a quarter for a meal. Fred swears Dean Celine was waiting for him at the end of the line with her hand out....after the servers had loaded his plate with food. We took many bus trips to 49th and North Avenue to eat pizza and garlic bread at Mama Mia's. Once in a while someone would get "pinned" and the frat guys would show up below her window to sing...that was excitement for all. The opening of Mayfair Shopping Mall was a real plus.

Other good friends included roommates Rose Vettese and Helen Walker. I waited eagerly each spring for our first warm day when traditionally Helen did a cartwheel on the driveway....as we were not supposed to wear anything but skirts off campus it was a challenge. Rolled up jeans under trench coats were popular. Rose was editor of the school paper and she and Helen, Carol Gill and I traveled to the Pfister Hotel to witness John Kennedy announce his run against Hubert Humphrey in the Wisconsin primary. We had our picture taken with the senator and Rose "interviewed" Jackie. She asked her if she set her hair in rollers. I had to laugh when a columnist from the Milwaukee Sentinel mentioned this in his column a number of years later. Neglecting to mention Kenneth, her famous hairdresser, Jackie very politely responded that rollers were used to set her hair. Most of the Kennedy family visited Mount Mary that year and we volunteered to help with his campaign. The senator carried the college vote, and Milwaukee, but Nixon took Wisconsin. For most of us it would be our first experience voting in a presidential election and it was an exciting time.

Those of us from "up north" rode the Chicago Northwestern "400" back and forth to Marinette and Menominee. It wasn't a bad trip except on Chicago/Green Bay football weekends when drunken Bear fans would think it a cute trick to land in our laps while staggering to the bathroom. Junior year a friend and neighbor said he would drive me home if I would take his car and load it with all my belongings. He was embarrassed to even try. All went well until I found it impossible to shift the VW Beatle into reverse. Faithful Helen offered to ride downtown with me to pick up John at city hall in Friday rush hour. She only had to get out twice and push me backward out of parking places.

Other highlights included our Junior Christmas play where the rising moon hit the roof, bounced down off the stage and back up to its correct position. It was not supposed to be a comedy. We held a costume contest on Halloween. Marching around the swimming pool in an assortment of costumes, way past lights out, was daring. My choice for best costume was Mary St. Peter's. She painted her face and hands, wore green clothing and had leaves growing out of her head.

We were given the opportunity to earn spending money by doing "scullery". You could either do lunch or breakfast and dinner which netted you a couple dollars a day. The camaraderie and song were probably worth as much or more. I still can sing, *My father slew a Kangaroo and he gave me the grisly part to chew. Now wasn't that a terrible thing to do? To give me to chew the grisly part of a dead kangaroo!*

We had holiday banquets when we dressed up in our best and ate by candlelight. On the last night before Christmas vacation, the seniors, in robes and pajamas, marched through the halls caroling. One year someone actually stole the baby Jesus figure and left the note, " In a little while you will no longer see Me; and again in a little while, you will see Me." The figure was returned and the culprit was never identified.

Graduation finally arrived and we looked forward to the tradition of step singing. The seniors, in cap and gown, marched with lanterns around the courtyard. As we began our rendition of "You'll Never Walk Alone" the skies opened up and the thunder boomed as we shouted, "Walk on through the wind, walk on through the rain." We were soaked by the time we retired to the plaid lounge in Notre Dame Hall to finish.

Step Singing before the Storm

In the last 56 years since graduation I have only missed 2 reunions celebrated every 5 years. We look forward to seeing each other, to singing "Mount Mary Here's to You," and waiting for Mary Lou Capodice Ross, class of '60, to shout at us in her husky voice, "See you in five years. Stay healthy. Eat Garlic!" I guess that is the Italian way and it's worked for her. Last year my daughter, president of the Illinois Occupational Therapy Association presented Mary Lou with an award for excellence in her field. She had just retired at 75.

DEDICATION

I dedicate this book to my family. Besides Dan and Lisa I write so that my grand-children Zack, Jake, Sydney, Carley and Kami will know what life was like when Grandma was young. I also write for my brother Bob and his wife Dina and their kids who, although they don't always remember what I remember, are a great audience.

ACKNOWLEDGEMENTS

I would like to thank everyone who helped me write these stories. Cousins Barbara, Richard, Paul, Tom, Jim, Susan and Mary B. all contributed their memories of grandparents and parents. My sister-in-law, Dina and friend Mary Lee were good proofreaders and I needed them frequently over these last couple years. My memoirs classmates were also appreciative and honest in their opinions and critiques.

Mary Lynn attended Mount Mary College earning a BA degree in English. She first taught at Preble High School where she met her husband Gene. They married in 1961 and had two children Lisa and Dan. Mary Lynn returned to school graduating from UW-Milwaukee in 1982 with a BS degree in Educational Psychology/ Counseling. She worked as a homebound teacher for the city of Green Bay for 17 years and was a counselor at St. Joseph Academy when it closed. She retired after 11 years at Northeast Wisconsin Technical College in 2001 where she served as the Returning Adult Services Counselor. Her last day of work was 9/11/01. A single parent workshop was meeting at the Salvation Army that evening. It was decided to bring their children from childcare into the workshop so that everyone could discuss their feelings about the tragedy that had occurred that morning. It was a therapeutic and memorable experience for all.

Mary Lynn also served as a Religious Education instructor for 25 years and is currently working on her second book.

Made in the USA
Lexington, KY
30 June 2017